George was born 12 August, .   ., in Southend-on-Sea, Essex and grew up in that area. After studying a number of therapies and having many life experiences he has decided to share some of them with you.

Some of the content may be hard to swallow at first, but it is very sincere and honest. Hopefully you will be inspired to see things differently after reading this book.

George F Bird

THINKING OUTSIDE THE BOX

Facing Up to the Truth About Life

AUSTIN MACAULEY PUBLISHERS™

LONDON • CAMBRIDGE • NEW YORK • SHARJAH

A CIP catalogue record for this title is available from the British Library.

ISBN 9781788484282 (Paperback)
ISBN 9781788484299 (ePub e-book)

www.austinmacauley.com

First Published (2021)
Austin Macauley Publishers Ltd
25 Canada Square
Canary Wharf
London
E14 5LQ

Table of Contents

Foreword

Let me introduce myself; I was born on 12 August 1946, in Southend-on-Sea, Essex and lived with my mum, dad and two older sisters in rented accommodation in the Southend area for the first 12 years of my life. Then my mum took on a mortgage (I said my mum because it was her that always made the big decisions in our lives, my dad just followed).

I became interested in music, particularly pop, and I started to learn to play the guitar at age 11. My influences were Elvis, Cliff Richard and the Shadows (at that time known as the Drifters) and most of the other popular singers and bands at that time.

At age 14, I, along with one of my sisters and some friends, started playing with an ouija board, and that was when I first realised that there is much more to this life than what we see with our eyes. At first, it was exciting; we were becoming aware of things and gaining knowledge about things which couldn't possibly be known without a connection to a higher intelligence.

We then experienced a very dark side, one which terrified us. And after a number of scary goings-on (which upset not only me, but my family as well), we were told that if we wore a cross, we would keep mischievous spirits away. So we did, and things seemed to calm down after that.

When I was 19, my mum had taken on a hairdresser's shop which one of my sisters ran, and I had the opportunity to join a local professional band. I was now, at last, doing what I thought I wanted to do for the rest of my working life.

Things went well and the band gained popularity, making a number of records and even achieving chart success (in Japan, of all places).

It was while working in that band that I was introduced to the Watchtower Bible and Tract Society, in other words, Jehovah's Witnesses. Most members of the band were involved in it, one way or another, and their beliefs made sense to me, especially as those beliefs made me feel protected, even to the point of taking off the cross I'd worn for the last five years (I was told that Jesus died on a stake, not a cross, and that the cross was contrary to the beliefs of Jehovah's witnesses).

I attended the meetings, became more and more involved, and eventually got baptised and went on to give a number of public talks to different congregations in the area.

At age 23, I was married, then two years later, along came my first child. It was at that time that I decided to make an effort to earn a regular, steady income and get what was then considered to be a proper job.

I used to enjoy driving, becoming a member of the Institute of Advanced Motorists at age 18, so I did the obvious thing at that time and trained to be a driving instructor.

After a while, I bought the business from the person I was working for and eventually started my own driving school. Being a driving instructor gave me a reasonable income for 28 years, during which time I built up a successful business and gave a number of lectures on safe driving.

It was also during that time that I had my second child. I was still a Jehovah's Witness and took my children to the meetings regularly, even though my wife only came along on occasions to please me.

What really appealed to me about Jehovah's Witnesses was the principle of loving your neighbour and your enemy, but what did not sit right with me was the belief that only Jehovah's Witnesses would be saved at the great Armageddon. So, along with that and a few other issues, and after missing the meetings for a while due to a back problem, I eventually drifted away.

Now many years down the line, I find that there are still many issues with Jehovah's Witnesses that do not feel right to me, however, it must be said, there are also many principles I still carry with me.

During this time, I also went back into the music business as a semi-professional (it is very rare for a musician to give it up completely; they say it's in the blood), and this continued in one way or another and still does right up until the present time.

You would have thought that being a driving instructor with a successful business and being a musician *and* having a young family would lead to complete contentment, but I felt unfulfilled because of my desire to help people.

In 1991 came a massive recession. My driving school business virtually collapsed, I lost my house and my marriage also folded. I ended up in a two-room rented flat with just one driving school car remaining, which brought me in just enough money to survive.

It was during this time that I met a lady who later became my partner. After a while, I moved into her house, and together we gained a good quality of life. She encouraged me in all my life's decisions and has continued to do so right up until the present time.

Incidentally, in 2018, she became my wife after 22 years of being my partner (I never did believe in rushing things).

Because my interest in being a driving instructor had severely waned, I took the bull by the horns, gave up that job and started training to be a therapist. I wanted to train as a psychologist, but finances at the time did not permit, so I went to night school and trained as a hypnotherapist.

Then came the thirst for more therapies; the study of magnetic therapy, energy therapy, oriental medicine, then finally after a visit to America, the study of blood and gene types and their connection with diet and disease.

During this time, I started a Complementary Clinic, then later a blood group diet clinic. I also gave a series of lectures and did a number of radio interviews.

My partner gave up her job and worked with me as a receptionist in the clinics and things were going very well, but I could not help feeling that I still was not completely fulfilled; I now had the tools to help people to improve the state of their body *and* their mind, but something was still missing.

I attempted to deal with this in my clinics and in my lectures, but I did not have a counselling qualification and to be honest, I didn't want one; surely wisdom gained through experience and inspiration is far more valuable than knowledge which is found by reading books.

Most therapists will agree that the knowledge found in the instruction manuals gets thrown out of the window as soon as you have your qualifications anyway—I remember clearly the words of my Shiatsu instructor on gaining my qualification, "You've got your qualification, now forget the theory and go out there and experience being a real therapist."

My therapy work was also interrupted by me officiating at my mother's funeral service at her request in 1997, then being asked to conduct subsequent funeral services, ending with me gradually doing my therapies less and less, and becoming a funeral service officiant.

My need to help people has been greatly fulfilled in this occupation, but I still feel the need to culminate everything I have learned and put it in an easy-to-understand language. My ultimate goal now is to help anyone who wants to listen, to change their lives for the better as I have been privileged to do in my life.

I have been very privileged to have learnt and understood what I now believe wholeheartedly to be the way to find lasting contentment, and I want to share it with you, so the first part of this book is to give you what I believe to be the answers to some burning questions which have continued to plague mankind from the very beginning.

This information is not only a culmination of what I have learnt over many years of having an inquisitive nature, it is probably mainly from inspiration that comes to me because I ask for it, and if it helps you then my work is done.

I have had the privilege to give a talk as a funeral service officiant to thousands of people over the years which is titled: *Is there such a thing as an Afterlife?* At some point in the not-too-distant future, I will not be in a position to give that talk anymore, so I want to share it with as many people as possible, not just now, but also after I leave this world behind (you will find the talk in chapter five of this book).

Please do not think that this is advice coming from someone who has perfected all the techniques you will read about. I am in the same boat as you, it's just that I am privileged to know how to find true contentment and I want to share it with you.

Introduction

Almost everything we say and do is influenced by us being controlled and manipulated. That seems to be a very rash statement, doesn't it? But think about it; how many of the things you say and do are purely generated from your own thoughts and desires, or how many are according to what you have been told or taught, or how you ought to behave?

Throughout this book, you will find many examples of typical behaviour which we tend to accept as normal. For example, what we are taught by our parents, what we are taught in school, what our peers tell us, what our employer tells us, what religions teach us, what the government says, what media we are exposed to and even what clothes we should wear. These are just a few examples of how we are expected to behave.

But just how much of this is right or correct and how much of it is just based on the opinions and beliefs of those who influence us? How much of this is simply us being controlled?

I implore you to re-examine your life to check if you are acting out your genuine preferences and desires, or whether you are following suit with the majority of society as to how you are expected to behave.

But to begin, let's answer some of the crucial questions that mankind has been asking over the centuries and never really had satisfactory answers to.

Chapter 1

Where Did It All Start and Where Will It End?

Where did it all start and where will it end? Perhaps it didn't start, and it won't end. That's right; perhaps life on this planet or indeed life anywhere in the universe never had a beginning or will never experience an end. I know that's hard to comprehend, but that's probably because we are human, and humans *do* experience time.

I would be very interested if you could show me even one example of something that has had an absolute beginning, something that started from absolutely nothing. I believe you could show me absolutely nothing.

If you could take a trip out into the universe and travel for a million or perhaps ten million light years, do you think you would see a brick wall? And even if you did, do you think there would be nothing behind it? Well, even if there was, nothingness is still made up of energy molecules. In other words, there is no such thing as nothingness.

Now take an inward journey, perhaps inside your body. Look at a single cell, then go in even further and look inside that cell and keep going. Do you think you would reach a point where there is nothing to see? No, actually you would reach a point where you would see a miniature universe, exactly like the giant one we see when we look out to the stars and planets at night. No beginning and no end.

Let us now take things a step further and talk about time. Everything in the past is nothing but a memory, and everything in the future is nothing more than a projection in our minds as to what might happen. But let us analyse that belief; if there is no such thing as a beginning or an end, would it not be reasonable then to believe that there's no past or future either?

What if everything from the so-called past and everything from the so-called future is all happening right now, but just on a different energy frequency? That would certainly explain why psychics and fortune tellers could know things that we believe haven't yet occurred.

It would also explain why we often get tuned in to things that happened in the so-called past. Perhaps those events were not in the past at all; perhaps they are all happening right now, but just on different energy frequencies. In other words, perhaps there is only the NOW, the PRESENT MOMENT. There is some interesting information on that very subject by Eckhart Tolle; his books are well worth a read.

Many years ago, Sir Albert Einstein made a discovery which has the potential to completely change the way we live our lives. That discovery was $E=Mc\sqrt{}$. Do you realise exactly what that means? It means that *everything* in this life (without exception), all consists of the same stuff; energy. There is actually no such thing as a solid object, just a mass of tightly packed energy molecules, the more solid a thing appears to be, the more energy molecules are packed into it.

On the other hand, there is no such thing as nothing, because even what we perceive to be nothing is still something. It is a group of energy molecules which are less tightly packed together than something which we consider to be tangible.

Of course, the density of the energy is not the only consideration. Just as important is the frequency (the level of oscillation, or if you prefer, vibration). Energy vibrates at many different frequencies, which include colour, smell, sound, and of course, light. And the highest energy frequency of all, the purest energy known to mankind has a name; that name is LOVE.

Throughout the course of this book, you will find the word energy mentioned many times. At first, I thought I had used this word too often, but then while considering the possibility of using other words to take its place, I decided that because this book is about nothing other than energy, and the whole of life consists of nothing more than energy, how can I *not* refer to it so many times?

Chapter 2
What Are We?

A very interesting question. As I mentioned earlier, we, along with literally everything else in this life, are nothing more than energy molecules vibrating at different rates and grouping in different densities, and that includes every part of us (even the invisible components such as our mind).

And because everything (including the air we breathe) is also made up of nothing more than energy molecules, there is actually no separation between things. It's an illusion to think that things are separate and distinct from each other.

Every action creates a reaction. Every cause has an effect. Everything you do makes an impression on everything else in this world. That is why we are all partially responsible for everything that happens.

So the secret to making our lives content is to resonate with the higher, purer energy. That way we will certainly experience the benefits, and as I said earlier; the purest energy known to mankind has a name and that name is LOVE. The more love you send out, the more love you receive, it's as simple as that.

There are some of those among us who know very well how to immerse themselves into the higher energies; for example, you can see it when you watch the Orientals doing Qi Gong exercises. You can see it when you watch healers working their magic on a sick or infirmed person. And you can probably see it, most of all, when you watch a mother with her newly born baby, or even when you look at a newly born kitten or puppy.

Also, there are those who rejuvenate their energies by doing such things as sitting in a forest, or even hugging a tree; some people I was travelling with once were laughing about someone who they saw hugging a tree, they thought he'd lost his marbles. I just kept quiet and thought my own thoughts; what a rejuvenating thing to do!

Because everything in this life is made of nothing more than energy molecules, it then naturally follows to believe that this life we lead is all an illusion. What your eyes take in is interpreted by your brain as being, for example, a tree or a house, but the truth is that we are only seeing energy vibrating at different rates and at different densities, so it's all just an illusion, it's all just our interpretation of what we see.

We put labels on different energy frequencies and densities, and call them trees or houses, but that's nothing more than a label, based upon what we've been led to believe. Not everyone sees the same thing when their brain interprets the light energy that enters their eyes.

So perhaps the time has come to stop judging people according to the way we have been taught to believe, and start accepting that nothing in this world is what it seems; to put it in the words of Zen Masters, 'What is, is, or it is what it is.' And you may as well learn to accept what is, because you won't change it anyway. Learn to change the things in your life that don't work for you and accept the things you can't change. Go with the flow and enjoy the ride.

The traditional Orientals also have a completely different way of seeing things with regard to our health and well-being. They understand the illusionary nature of our lives, so they tend not to label illnesses. For example, where our healthcare professionals would diagnose a person with an illness such as hypertension or heart disease (in other words, put a label on the illness), then treat the symptoms with chemical drugs, the traditional Orientals consider all illness to be nothing more than disturbed energy flow and attempt to re-balance the person's bio-energy, rather than labelling the disease and trying to treat the symptoms.

Chapter 3

Who Are We?

Throughout the pages of this book, I will be making a number of controversial statements, some of which you may find hard to accept, perhaps they will even offend you. But I ask you to please give these statements careful consideration before you dismiss them.

So let's start this chapter by getting the first one out of the way; "Perhaps there is no such thing as an evil person." I know that statement will offend many people, but it has to be said.

The first response to that statement, whenever I make it, is usually something like; "How can you say there is no such thing as an evil person when there are people in this world who are happy to kill and maim just for the sake of religion?" or "How can you make such a statement when there are people in this world who seem to get pleasure out of hurting, abusing or even killing others?"

Please notice; I did not say there is no such thing as evil deeds, I said there is no such thing as an evil *person*. The problem is that some people have lost their way. Perhaps they have stopped listening to the gentle promptings of their soul.

You have a choice in everything you decide to do. The soul does not take you over or control you, but it does have a way of gently prompting you, and this is done by way of your conscience. The conscience is something we all have, it's just that sometimes we push it right into the background and ignore it, but you cannot destroy it. It will always be there if you choose to listen to it.

Sometimes people ignore their conscience for so long that it becomes natural for them to carry out wicked deeds. That doesn't mean *they* are evil. It just means they have lost the connection with their soul and gone down a different path.

Everyone has the ability to change direction though, sometimes it is when they lose a loved one, or perhaps when they get so low that they wonder what life is all about, and sometimes it's when a past memory triggers that re-connection with their soul.

Everyone has the right to change their ways, in fact, sometimes a person who has changed from doing wicked deeds to becoming compassionate is even more loved than someone who has always been compassionate.

So, let's see if we can understand the complicated workings of the human mind. Let's start by saying; we are all born innocent, in fact, if we weren't born innocent, we couldn't be blamed for the way we behave anyway.

So if we agree that we were all born innocent, then at what point of time in the life of a person who does evil things, do you think that he or she began to become evil? Are you saying that it was entirely their choice and that no-one else had a hand in it? I think you know that's not true.

As we grow up, we are all influenced by the environment we live in and we are all partly responsible for the evil which prevails in this world, even though our personal part in it may be small. No one person is fully responsible for the evil deeds we see. We are all connected and therefore we are all partly responsible; hence there is no such thing as an evil person, there are only people who do evil things.

That brings us to the next controversial statement: there is no such thing as pure evil. The only thing in this world that is totally pure is LOVE. Everything else is a mixture of positive and negative, yin and yang, even though the balance may heavily swing one way or the other in differing circumstances.

But the big question still remains: who are we? When we speak of our body parts, we refer to them, for example, as my arm, my leg, my heart or my head. Yet when we refer to our whole body, rather than say my body, we usually say 'me'. Who *is* me? Are we whole (including our soul, our personality, and even our mind)?

When we say my arm or my leg, who is the *me* we are referring to? Is it our personality or our soul? When we see someone we know, we usually say, "there's John, or there's Susan," but exactly which part of John or Susan are we referring to; their body, their mind, their personality, which?

Perhaps the soul enters the body at birth in order to experience human life and all that comes with it, and the person we become (our traits, qualities and tendencies) is the development of our mind or ego.

Our ego can go in many different directions, and the soul simply goes for the ride. But if the soul is pure and innocent

23

as we are led to believe, then perhaps it tries to prompt us when we are acting in an unloving or foolish way. So when we act in a loving and compassionate way, our soul is pleased and we feel that pleasure by way of contentment.

We all know what it means to live a loving and compassionate life, but unfortunately, the mind (or ego, if you prefer to call it that) does everything possible to lead us towards gaining attention for ourselves, and that process starts very soon after birth (you only have to watch the behaviour of a young child who wants sweets or a toy to see this in action).

Throughout life, we are either completely led by our ego, or we remain aware of the workings of the ego and stay in control. If you have been led somewhat by your ego, there's always the opportunity to change things, to get back in the driver's seat, so to speak.

But keep in mind this one thing: when you attempt to change for the better; the ego doesn't like it, it wants to keep getting the attention, so it will make things rather difficult for you until it eventually realises that its efforts are futile.

So be strong, refuse to allow your ego to rule you, and you will certainly feel the benefits by way of contentment. Keep talking to yourself (probably one of the first signs of sanity in this crazy world).

And on that subject, I am going to make another one of those controversial statements. Here goes: everything you say (that is except when you are furnishing someone with some necessary information) is for the purpose of gaining attention for yourself. Yes, every time you open your mouth and speak (except when you are assisting someone), it is your ego trying to gain attention. So with that in mind, the less opinions we have about anything, the better it will be.

Many spiritual writers tell us that we are simply a product of our own actions. They tell us that the person we have become and the pain and illness we suffer is all because of the way we have been thinking.

Personally, I cannot fully accept that theory. I do accept that many, or maybe even most of the problems we experience, have been brought on by us and what we believe, but I can't accept that it applies to everything. For example, you can't say that a person is personally responsible for their suffering when they have been born with a genetic disease. You can't say a person is responsible when they happen to suffer from a natural disaster or get struck down by an unexpected illness.

Clearly our lives are a combination of circumstances, and we have a certain amount of control over the outcome. For example, if you smoke 50 cigarettes a day and then develop lung cancer, it's no use saying, "why me?" Clearly, *we* are fully responsible for most things that happen in our lives.

Chapter 4

Why Are We Here?

There have been many books written on this subject, and if you believed everything that is written, you would be in a state of total confusion. Interestingly, I believe we are *already* in a state of confusion.

Some believe that we just happened to come about by chance, and for those cases there is no explanation required, because there would be absolutely no purpose to life anyway.

Others believe that there is a divine purpose, and we are simply living out a planned existence. I do not believe we are living out a totally planned existence; otherwise we would never need to take any precautions, because if we did, it would make no difference anyway. For example, why look before you cross the road if your time of death is already pre-determined?

I don't believe the soul exercises that much control. Take, for example, catastrophes of a massive nature such as earthquakes, tsunamis or hurricanes; are we expected to believe that all those thousands of people have been manoeuvred into that place at that time just to experience the end of their incarnation? No, I don't accept the 'When your number's up' theory.

Still, others believe we have choices to make, and our after-life future depends upon how we have lived our lives, rather like a point-scoring process.

What do I believe? I believe we have a soul, and the purpose of our incarnation is for our soul to experience human life; that means experiencing everything this life throws at us.

I believe we have a certain amount of control over our destiny, and that we should show respect to our body and take reasonable precautions to protect ourselves from danger, but I also believe we can take this too far.

If we spend our lives worrying about what might happen, we will miss out on the enjoyment of life. It's a case of balance; why not take reasonable steps to look after yourself, and at the same time take a few minor risks and enjoy some excitement? Life would be very boring if we just spent it in a cocoon of self-protection.

One way in which it is beneficial to look after ourselves is by the way we treat our body. As I mentioned earlier, it is good to take reasonable steps in order to look after our body, and a good way of doing this is by monitoring the food we eat.

There is a lot to be learnt about the fact that different people would benefit by eating a diet which suits them. One way to do this is to eat according to our blood and gene type. Much research has been done on the subject and it is amazing how much better people feel when they eat food that is compatible with their blood and gene types.

This is a subject though that one could devote a whole book to, and in fact have done, so rather than going into detail here, I suggest you look at the work of Peter D'Adamo and his father, James D'Adamo, on the fascinating subjects of how diet and disease are connected with your blood and gene types.

And before we move on to the next topic, I must point out the importance of drinking pure, clean water; your body and mind will not function properly if you are dehydrated. I used to think that I only needed to drink water if I was thirsty. Wrong. Since I dramatically increased my water intake, I have functioned so much better in every way.

Exercise is another important factor if we want to keep our bodies reasonably healthy. Some like vigorous, challenging exercise, and some (me included) prefer a more subtle type; I believe the most important thing is movement, so I engage in Qi Gong exercises almost every morning; it keeps my joints from ceasing up, while at the same time keeping my bio-energy flowing smoothly.

One of the joints, which is usually the first to cease up, is the sacroiliac joint in the lower spine. Most elderly people have lost flexibility in this joint, but Qi Gong exercises have so far kept this joint mobile, for me at least.

If you wish to include Qi Gong in your daily regime, you will find numerous videos on YouTube. The techniques differ slightly, but whatever form you use, I feel it would be another good tool for helping you stay physically and spiritually fit.

But also keep in mind that none of the above advice will have any real effect if you don't get adequate sleep. In this modern society, it seems that everything continues on a 24-

hour basis, there's always something to do at any time of the day or night, but if we rob ourselves of one of our most basic needs (sleep), we will never be able to enjoy the benefits of any of the above advice.

Now let's talk about another important, but powerful factor in our lives; the desire for sex. Sex is probably the most powerful need we have, second to food and water. Why is this so? Simply because if we didn't have such a strong desire for sex, the human race might stop reproducing, culminating in the lack of human bodies for souls to incarnate into.

So don't be ashamed of your desire for the opposite sex, it is one of the most natural desires in our lives, which I believe is there for a purpose, but be careful of how you exercise that desire, because it could cause you and others much heartache if you allow your animal instincts to just run riot.

So to sum up the answer to the question 'Why are we here?' my answer is simply this; we are here to provide a vehicle for the soul to experience life as a human. We are not here to learn anything; our soul already knows everything, and that knowledge is openly available to you if you care to look for it.

We are here to experience happiness and sadness, pain and pleasure, so why not enjoy life in the process, enjoy the ride?

Chapter 5

What Happens When We Die?

This is a talk I usually give at a funeral service. Over the centuries, there have been many theories put forward in an attempt to answer to this question, and I believe the truth is that nobody can say with any accuracy what the answer actually is. However, I would like to put forward an explanation which is scientific, an explanation which hopefully no-one can argue with, and happily the scientific explanation goes some way to giving hope as to the existence of an after-life.

There are two scientific facts I would like to draw your attention to; the first is that everything in this life, without exception, and I mean everything (including the body we live in) is all made of the same stuff; energy, nothing more.

The second scientific fact I would like to share with you is one I hope you will draw some comfort from: energy cannot die. Another proven scientific fact is that you could not destroy even one single particle of energy, however much you tried (scientists have been trying to do it for years).

So, if energy doesn't die, and our body is made of energy, what happens to it? The answer is that it simply changes form. Nothing in this life ceases to exist, it merely changes form. So, the question 'What is death?' is easily answered with one simple word; 'change'.

We are made up of many different frequencies and densities of energy; from the densest, our body, right up to the higher forms of energy, the personality and the characteristics, the real person living inside that body, the person people know.

And there comes a time in everyone's life, as you well know, when that body can no longer support us, so the body's energy changes form. That doesn't mean we cease to exist as I stated earlier, nothing in this life ceases to exist.

I believe that the higher energies (the personality, the characteristics, the higher self) continue on as ever before, so, just because you can't see or touch somebody whose body has ceased to function, it doesn't mean they cease to exist, it just means they no longer live inside that body.

There are many different beliefs about the after-life; many people who have been close to death appear to go through a tunnel of light, and meet up with the loved-ones who went before them (you might refer to it as being in Heaven). But where is Heaven? If we are to believe organised religion, we would believe that Heaven is a wonderful place, a paradise where selected souls float up to and roam around in total happiness and contentment.

Well, if that's the case, then why do souls want to leave Heaven and incarnate into human existence? Surely, they'd be better off staying where they are and enjoying total peace and contentment.

No, I believe that Heaven isn't a place at all, but a parallel existence right here with us, running on a different frequency to the human one, alongside many other existences that we believe to be past and future.

Another belief (particularly in the Eastern world) is that we continue to re-incarnate until we reach a certain level of spiritual development or enlightenment.

What do I believe? I'm sorry if I disappoint you here but the truth is, I don't know. I do feel certain though that life continues on in some way, and I believe our soul is eternal (science actually backs up that belief) but as to the exact process, I don't know the answer, and I have a suspicion that no one else will know either, that is, of course, until their time comes.

Surely the important thing though is to take each day as it comes and not concern ourselves with the future, but instead to live this life in such a way that we find contentment and peace, and I do believe I know how we can do that.

Chapter 6
Who Is God?

The difficult thing about this subject is determining what the word God means to you. Is your God a person, a person who watches over everything in this world and makes judgements as to how to deal with His people according to their behaviour? Is your God a jealous God who punishes people for not giving their devotion exclusively to Him? Or is your God loving, kind and forgiving?

My God is not a person at all. My God is LOVE. The energy that makes up this wonderful universe is an intelligent energy, a powerful loving force that is there for the benefit of anyone who wishes to connect with it.

My God operates by the power of attraction; the quality of the energy you give out resonates with the quality of the energy you receive. So you could call it a form of karma, but this is not to be confused with the belief that you will be punished if you perform wicked deeds. I believe there is no punishment, but if the energy that you give out is negative then you will have brought upon yourself more negativity. That's how the law of attraction works. The universe is like a mirror; what you give out is what you receive, and what you receive is what you yourself have created, not punishment from some judgemental God, but a reflection of the natural laws of attraction.

The chapter entitled *Examples of everyday giving with love* is there to show you how you can take full advantage of the natural laws of attraction and make your life content. It really does work, but it is not so simplistic that you can have anything you want, whenever you want it. You need to understand how the law of attraction works, and if you think you can use it for selfish reasons, you will be greatly disappointed.

Chapter 7

A Word About Evolution

Charles Darwin changed the way the world thinks. Before him, it was the accepted thing to believe in some sort of Deity, some superior power. Then along came Darwin who gave people the excuse to behave in any way they wanted, because they now believed that they did not have to answer to anyone or anything. They were told that survival of the fittest was all there is.

And they believed it; church attendances diminished, crimes rose, and selfishness and greed became the new way forward. 'Get what you can out of this world and don't worry if someone suffers in the process'; that became the new way of thinking.

So, did everything really happen by mere chance? Was there absolutely no intelligent force behind the amazing things that happen in this world? Do you really believe that? I certainly don't.

I think there is confusion about certain aspects of evolution. The part of evolution that is called adaptation seems to be where one problem lies. Of course, things adapt to their environment, it is part of the wonderful process of life on this planet. But do you really believe that these adaptations occur blindly, without intelligent thought?

And what about the process of life itself? Do you believe that a baby is conceived in the womb by blind chance, and that every time a woman conceives, it is purely by luck?

And another question: if we evolved from apes as we are led to believe, where are the half-formed humans? We have apes and we have humans, so if evolution was a truth and not merely a theory (and a weak one at that), where are the creatures that are still in the stages of development? You can't have fully formed apes and fully formed humans without the in-between creatures.

It was once suggested by evolutionists that Australian Aborigines were the missing link, so an Aborigine, who was unable to read or spell, was taken from his native environment and taken to America as an experiment, to see if he could be educated. Guess what; after a while, he not only learnt to read and write, he also came away with qualifications; hardly an example of a half-formed human.

One other thing is that if we evolved from lower creatures over millions of years, and we are the top of the evolutionary tree so to speak, how come creatures from the so-called lower end of life constantly teach us lessons?

There are myriads of examples about how we constantly learn new things by observing these so-called lower creatures that can achieve things that we wouldn't even be able begin to accomplish (a few of these examples can be found in the chapter called *Why Do Bad Things Happen?*)

Chapter 8

Are There Such Things As Evil Spirits?

Just as I don't believe there is such a thing as an evil person, neither do I believe in the existence of evil spirits. However, there are many people who would argue against that because of the experiences they've had and the many people who fervently believe in the existence of Satan.

Just as I don't believe that God is a person, neither do I believe Satan is either. Personally, I've had very unpleasant experiences with what I believed to be evil spirits in the past, after dabbling with ouija boards and the like. Many non-believers would say, 'That is nothing more than your own mind, creating fear.' Well, I find that difficult to accept because of the experiences I've had, so I am forced to believe that there are spirits who have mischievous tendencies and, in the process, get some sort of pleasure from creating fear in humans.

Perhaps there are different levels in the spirit world, the lower the level, the least developed they are. Perhaps there is a process of development that continues until perfection or enlightenment is achieved.

Whatever your belief, I feel sure that the highest, purest energy in this life is love, and that love is always there to guide and protect you, whenever you need it. I also believe that nothing is powerful enough to overcome love, so follow what you know in your heart to be right and trust the love of the universe to see you through.

Chapter 9

Why Do Bad Things Happen?

You might well ask: if God is so loving and kind, why do terrible things such as earthquakes, tsunamis and hurricanes happen in this world? Or why did my loved one, who was so kind and loving, die in such tragic circumstances?

These are questions which have been asked many times throughout mankind's history, and in fact, questions which have led to a lack of faith and many people turning completely against God. How can anyone expect to remain faithful when they are told by organised religion that their loved one was taken from them by God, but without an explanation as to why? They are then made even more angry and frustrated when they are told to have faith.

Let's start firstly by repeating that God is not a person, but a powerful, loving force. So why would a powerful loving force allow these tragedies to happen?

This earth on which we live is very intelligent. Yes, that's right; there *is* intelligence outside of the brain. Your body is intelligent; when did you ever have to worry about how to survive when your body is threatened by a deadly virus or bacteria? When did you ever have to think about how to heal a wound or repair a broken bone?

Medical scientists have yet to realise that our body has the capability of sorting out its own problems without you even having to think about how the process works, and believe me, the process is far more complex than we, or in fact any medical expert, would even have a hope of understanding. Our body constantly makes adjustments of its own accord in order to keep things in balance.

It amazes me, for example, how, particularly in the western world, the medical profession prescribes many chemical-based drugs, one example being a drug which is a poison (Digoxin, taken from digitalis, the leaves of the foxglove plant and which is highly poisonous to humans). This drug slows down the heart by administering poison to it. That is only one example as there are many other chemical drugs which are prescribed for a myriad of health problems. Why don't the medical profession just investigate the cause of the problem and recommend changes to diet and lifestyle, instead of simply addressing the symptoms? Why don't they holistically support the body, rather than try to fight the disease?

Admittedly, there are times when our body does need a little help to resolve a health problem, but the sad thing is that this is usually because we have created the problem in the first place and caused confusion.

How do we expect our body to cope when we constantly abuse it in so many ways; with the chemicals we ingest in what we eat and drink, with the polluted air we breathe, with the constant bombardment of electro-magnetic fields, with the radio signals we are receiving in almost every corner of the earth now, with the radiation we are exposed to in modern day lighting and microwaves and with the relentless stress which life in this modern world forces us to endure?

And that's not to mention the chemical drugs we ingest which are labelled as cures, all with side effects that often cause us even more damage than the condition we took them for in the first place. Many people, particularly the elderly, are prescribed a massive cocktail of drugs to take every day, and most of those drugs are often just attempts to deal with the side-effects of the drugs they were taking in the first place. No wonder our bioenergy gets thrown off kilter.

I personally know of sickly people who stopped all their medication and felt better almost instantly (please don't think I'm suggesting that you take it upon yourself to stop your medication, you would need the support of a sympathetic healthcare professional).

So what about this wonderful planet on which we live? As I stated earlier, the earth, in fact the whole universe is ultra-intelligent. For example, did you know that when a colony of ants want to cross a river, they group into a large ball, trapping air inside, then they roll into the river on a bend, so that they reach the other side with the flow of the current, and only a small amount on the outside of the ball perishes. Do they have a brain?

What about the bird called the arctic turn; did you know that it can navigate thousands of miles using the stars, and even if only one star is visible, it can still pinpoint exactly where to fly? Even the domestic pigeon can find its way home when it is taken hundreds of miles away in a vehicle.

And one other example; do you realise just how far salmon travel when they go back to their spawning ground, even managing to jump upstream to get there?

These were just a few examples of how much intelligence there is on this planet alone, without the need of a human brain interfering, and there are myriads more.

The universe needs to make constant adjustments in order to continue to survive, and just like the ants crossing the river, it inevitably leads to, a small few by comparison, perishing.

Those adjustments come in the form of what we call natural disasters. Well, that is how we interpret them, but the disaster would be colossal if these adjustments weren't made. We wouldn't experience the death of a few hundred, or even a few thousand people, we would experience the death of the planet and everything on it. Everything happens for a reason, and the universe wouldn't allow anything to happen without good reason.

And please remember, nothing ever dies, and that includes us, so there is no such thing as the ultimate sacrifice.

Chapter 10

How Can We Find Contentment?

Many books have been written advising us on how to be happy, and that concept has always been difficult for me to comprehend. How can we become totally happy? However grounded, calm or laid-back we learn to become, we can't possibly avoid the causes of unhappiness. We can't stop the sadness we feel when a loved one is sick or dies, we can't stop how unhappy we feel when things beyond our control cause us to lose our possessions, or when someone we love experiences heartache.

No, the truth is that it is a natural thing to suffer sadness as part of our journey through this life. How can we really know what true happiness is if we haven't experienced sadness? So the state I believe we should be looking for is not happiness, but contentment. Yes, it is possible to experience contentment even when we are feeling sad or unhappy.

Contentment is not a state of constant happiness (which I honestly believe is impossible to achieve), it is a state of peace, and it is possible to be in a state of peace, regardless of our state of happiness or sadness.

The understanding of Yin and Yang sums this up perfectly; life is a constant flux of Yin and Yang; sun and moon, left and right, dark and light, happiness and sadness, negative and positive.

If you try to seek only the positive, you will have no grounding; take, for example, the illustration of a battery. If you only connect to the positive side, you will have no complete circuit to start your car or turn on your torch. If you connect a light bulb to the positive wire only, it couldn't work because both positive and negative are required in order to complete the circuit.

That's why we are here; not to experience only happiness, but to experience contentment through a combination of happiness and sadness, positive and negative.

So the point of this book is not to help you achieve a state of complete happiness, but to help you achieve a state of contentment. How can this be done? It can be easily summed up with just three words: GIVE WITH LOVE.

Remember, I said earlier that the universe is a mirror, and we receive according to what we give out. But this needs to be expanded upon in a practical way, a way which can help you to gradually achieve contentment over a period of time, a way in which we can embark on a program of changing our lives in gradual, easy steps.

The more you give with love, the more contentment you will feel. If we hold any grievance or grudge against someone, our level of contentment will therefore be limited, and that leads me to make a statement which some will accept, some will find difficult to accept, and some will refuse to accept, and if that applies to you, you will possibly stop reading this book at this point. However, it is what I sincerely believe, so it is something I feel we must learn to accept, even if we can't put it into practice yet.

Here's that statement: 'If you don't forgive everyone for everything they have ever done to you, you will never find complete contentment.'

The good news though is that contentment comes in levels, it's not something you have or don't have. The more people you can learn to forgive, the more contentment you will feel. The more you give with love, the less grievances you will have and the more contented you will feel.

And that's the secret; it's not just the giving, it's the *giving with love* that counts. It's your intention. For example, if you give someone your time and feel stressed the whole time you are with them because you are thinking about something you would rather be doing, you will not gain contentment from giving in that way. But if you give them your time in a kind and compassionate way, you will certainly feel contented because you will be giving with love.

If you just make an effort in some small way to give with love (even to a complete stranger), you will get that feel-good factor and experience a degree of contentment. So one of the purposes of this book is to help you to go through many ways in which you can start thinking about giving with love, and as a result, you will feel the joy of contentment, until maybe one day you will feel complete contentment because you live your life in a totally giving way and you hold a grievance or grudge against no one in this world.

Of course, as humans I'm not sure anyone will ever reach that perfect state, one thing I'm sure of is that we can get very close to it, and even if we barely begin to feel contented, the quality of our life will have changed for the better.

So let's start by looking at the many ways you can give with love. You may wish to make it a challenge for the week to make a point of seeing how you can do this in a practical way, or you may prefer to have a thought for the day and have it in your mind to apply it wherever you go that day. Whichever way you do it, you will get that feel-good factor more and more as the days go by.

However, as you do this, keep one thing in mind; the feel-good factor you experience when you give should not be confused with ego massaging. This is explained perfectly by Jesus in Matthew 6:2 and 3 when he said; 'When you do a charitable deed, do not sound a trumpet before you as the hypocrites in the synagogues and in the streets do, that they may have glory from men. But when you do a charitable deed, do not let your left hand know what your right hand is doing.'

Chapter 11

Happiness Versus Contentment

Happiness may be something which is out of your control, but contentment is not. We do not have to rely on other people to make us content; we can choose to be content. At this point you may be thinking, I didn't want this bad thing to happen to me and I certainly can't be happy under such circumstances. That is absolutely true, but let us not confuse happiness with contentment; they are two entirely different things; you can't be happy if you have just heard some sad news, but you can still be content.

It has been estimated that the average adult has approximately 60,000 to 80,000 thoughts per day, of which as much as 80% are negative. Do we have any control over this or is it just something we have to live with?

I believe that the most important thing with regard to our thought processes is HOW WE END EACH THOUGHT. For example, let's take a typical scenario; what you plan to do today. You could look at it negatively: The weather is bad. I feel tired. I don't have anyone to go with. The list can be endless. You have now set your day up to be negative and unless by some chance something very positive happens, it may go from bad to worse.

Now let's look at the positive scenarios: Whatever the weather, I can still enjoy my life. My positive outlook will energise me completely and dispel any tiredness I feel. I don't need to rely on someone else in order to be content; I make my own contentment.

Chapter 12

Giving with Love

Time

In this busy world that we live in, time is probably one of the least available commodities. We never seem to have enough of it, so the thought of giving away more time just for the pursuit of someone else's pleasure may seem to be a difficult thing.

But what about the time have already spent? Could it not have been better used to benefit others? For example, why not telephone someone who's feeling lonely, instead of spending wasted time watching TV programs that only stimulate negativity? I'm not saying it's wrong to have leisure time, we all need that. What I am saying though is that we would feel so much better if we made someone in need feel a little better by giving them some of our time.

Attention

When you are having a conversation with someone, either face-to-face or on the telephone, why not make a point of spending more time listening to what they have to say, and less time trying to put your point of view forward, trying to convince them that what you believe is right? Giving less attention to our ego and more attention to others will certainly make us feel more satisfied in the end, and it will make them feel better to know that someone is interested in what they have to say.

Gifts

Your first reaction to this suggestion might be: 'My life is a struggle to survive financially as it is, let alone spending money I don't have on someone else.'

I'm sure you have a number of items you rarely ever use. I'm also sure that there will be plenty of people less fortunate than yourself who would be overwhelmed at being given something out of pure kindness.

According to the natural laws of this loving universe which I mentioned earlier, the more you give, the more you will receive. If you give out of your surplus, you are doing a kindness, but if you give something by way of a sacrifice purely out of love and compassion, you could receive not only the equivalent of everything you gave, but also ten times more. That principle was brought out by Jesus Christ and has certainly proved to be true for me and many other people: 'Give to him that asketh thee, and from him that would borrow from thee, turn not thou away' (Matt 5:42).

Smiling

I don't, for one moment, suggest that you smile at everyone you come into contact with; you would soon get a reputation for being rather strange. Neither do I suggest you smile at an attractive stranger of the opposite sex if they are with their partner. That's not to say you shouldn't smile at strangers, it's a nice thing to do, just be selective and alert to the possible reaction.

Also, if you give a nice warm smile to a person you are in contact with in your everyday life such as a salesperson or a customer, it makes them (and you) feel good.

And never forget to smile often at those who are close to you, it has the immediate effect of calming a potentially explosive situation and certainly makes for a better relationship with them.

Touching

This way of giving is probably one of the areas where you need to be the most selective. However, it should be realised that there is not nearly enough touching taking place in this world today. People need to be touched, it's a natural need we all have, and life is very lonely without it.

It should obviously go without saying that you don't just go up to a complete stranger and touch them, but if a stranger is, for example, going through a trauma, it can be very comforting and re-assuring if you just place your hand on the back of their shoulder or gently hold their arm.

Shaking hands with a person you come into contact with is also a good form of touching which usually brings positive results.

Hugging is another way of touching which makes people feel that they are cared for. It is now customary for people of both sexes to greet or say goodbye to someone they are fond of with a nice tight hug.

Also, try touching those you love more often, just a light touch as they walk past, you will make them feel wanted and make them feel you are thinking about them, and sometimes just hold them close to you in a warm embrace without saying a single word, it speaks volumes.

Kissing

Kissing is of course another form of touching, and it must be said that it is probably one of the most intimate, so a great deal of discretion is needed here. Having said that though, kissing is something we can often put into practice with many different people, and it can also create a very powerful way of giving if it is used in the right way.

When you are introduced to a person of the opposite sex, it is now customary to give them a kiss on the cheek or as in most continental countries, a kiss on both cheeks. Sometimes a kiss on the top of the head to someone who you are quite close to is a nice way of showing affection without giving offence.

Of course, the kiss on the lips is something which should only be reserved for your partner or someone very close to you. Why not do it more often and make them feel special? It helps you to feel good and them to feel wanted.

Giving Practical Help

There are few things more satisfying than being given a hand to complete a job of work which is becoming too much to handle, or a job which seems to be a mammoth task. On the other hand though, there could be a very small gesture which is easy to execute, such as helping an old or infirm person cross the road, or perhaps carrying shopping for someone who finds it difficult.

You may wish to offer your services to a charity or volunteer your spare time by helping out in a practical way at a hospital or elderly person's home.

In your home environment, you may wish to offer to help your partner or a family member with one of the chores which you don't usually attend to. It will be much appreciated and will contribute towards a harmonious life, and to your surprise, you might even find that you are also offered help with your chores. It's amazing how well people respond to kindness.

Showing Appreciation

There is nothing nicer than being appreciated for what you've done, so if you want to make someone feel worthwhile, why not show them your appreciation with a simple thank you?

Of course, showing appreciation isn't just by what you say, you can show appreciation in many ways; doing something for them in return, giving them a gift, giving them a kiss (of an appropriate nature), or even just simply saying thank you. All these things show you care and, in the long run, add to your level of contentment.

Giving Praise

This is not just saying thank you, it is commending the other person for their qualities. All too often, we take people for granted and expect a certain standard, but we would do well to ask ourselves; do I give praise to people as much as I expect praise to be given to me? Do I make kind comments about the way people in my life present themselves? Do I tell them how kind they are and how much I appreciate them for what they do and who they are? If you make a point of giving praise, you may be surprised at how well your comments are received, and you may also be surprised at how warm people can become in return.

Forgiveness

Probably the hardest thing for most people. This is the core of most problems in this world. Your natural reaction might be: why should I forgive her or him when they have caused so much pain in my life? Well, peace has to be worked for and it can't be achieved until someone makes the first move.

My philosophy used to be that I would gladly forgive someone if they showed remorse or asked me for forgiveness. But what if they don't? Are you going to spend the rest of your life ignoring them, or worse still, trying to get revenge because of the hurt they have caused you or your loved ones?

If this is the case, have you not considered the fact that you are partially responsible for the negative attitude prevailing in this world today? Are you aware that you have set yourself up as a judge of that person and by doing so suggested that you are better than them?

You could ask yourself why you think you have the right to judge others, because we all fall short of perfection in one way or another. Jesus Christ made a very powerful statement when a crowd of people were about to stone a prostitute, he said, 'let the one without sin cast the first stone.'

If you find it difficult to forgive, don't worry, you are probably amongst the majority of people on this planet. The main thing though is that you recognise the need to forgive and start somewhere; how about right now, even though it may be difficult?

Forgiving is not always something you say, in fact, sometimes it's not appropriate to say to someone, 'I forgive you' because they may feel they've done nothing wrong in the first place, so that could spark off even more problems.

Sometimes forgiving is carried out by just being nice to someone you feel has offended you. They may ask you why you are suddenly treating them differently, so you might say something like, 'I just think there's already too much negativity in this world and I don't want to add to it. Shall we just forget the past and move on from here?' You might be pleasantly surprised at how well that may be received, and regardless of the response, you will certainly feel more content with who you are.

As I stated earlier, you will never know contentment if you don't forgive. Refusing to forgive not only blocks love energy from flowing, but it also sets a barrier between yourself and the person you are refusing to forgive. In a nutshell, it separates you, and separation is another word for duality (something I will deal with later).

Be encouraged by the words of Jesus, when he said, 'Blessed are the merciful, for they will be shown mercy.' (Matthew 5:7)

Showing Compassion

If you are compassionate by nature, this should be an easy one for you. If you are not, it would now be a good time to start thinking about how you can show compassion to others. The best way to do this is by starting to think about caring more for others. There is great satisfaction in knowing you have shown compassion to those less fortunate than yourself, and you can do that in any of the ways discussed above.

Giving Sympathy

Sometimes being sympathetic is a case of just being there and saying nothing. There is much power in the presence of a kind person when you are feeling lost or devastated. Probably the worst thing you can say at a time like this is, 'I know how you feel'. The truth is you don't, so just being there at a time like this is usually sufficient. If they want to talk, then let them. The less you say, the better it will be.

Showing Empathy

Being able to put yourself in the other person's shoes. Being able to feel their pain as if it were you who were feeling it. Trying to understand what it feels like to be in their situation. If you are able to do this, you are in an excellent position to give them comfort and help them to deal with their situation, and by doing this, you will feel extremely fulfilled.

Promoting Peace

This is probably one of the most important things to be considered. Peace and contentment come together as a package. You can't be peaceful if you don't have contentment and you can't experience contentment if you aren't peaceful. The more peaceful you become, the more content you will be. How can you become more peaceful? By applying all the things discussed in this book.

Have you decided it's time to give with love more? Giving with love is the only way we can promote peace. You may, at this stage, use the argument that you can be peaceful by shutting out the world and becoming a recluse, therefore, having absolutely no involvement in the unrest of this world. But what you would be forgetting is that if nobody showed care and compassion then nobody would feel wanted, and that alone would lead to a frustrated life, hardly one you could call contented.

I repeat; you cannot experience true contentment if you don't give with love. It's that simple, so why not start today by making an effort to gradually learn to give with love more and more, and in the process gain the deep-rooted feeling of contentment that will certainly flow through you.

And as you give, remember; it's not what you say, or even what you do that counts, it is what you intend. Remember that the universe is a giant mirror. The more you intend love toward people, the more love you will receive.

Exercises

My original intention was to put together 365 exercises, one for each day of the year—a new one to take with you every day of the week; exercises which, if put into practise, will help your life to become fulfilled and contented.

However, after thinking about the practicality of this, I realised that it couldn't work; there are always going to be a number of days throughout every year when, for differing reasons, you just can't sit up in bed in the morning and read your exercise for the day. This would probably then lead to frustration, perhaps trying to catch up, then getting behind and possibly ending up by dropping the whole idea altogether.

The other problem with having an exercise for every day is that it doesn't have time to properly sink in before the next day's exercise takes place, by which time you may well have forgotten yesterday's exercise.

So I then decided to put together 50 exercises, one for each week. But the problem with that, is that everyone is different; there are some people who would achieve their goal on a particular exercise in just one day, some a week, others might need months to feel ready to move on to the next exercise, and still others may not even need to work on a particular exercise, because they've already accomplished it before reading this book.

So now, I've simply listed a number of exercises, to complete in your own time before moving on to the next one. Time is irrelevant here, so let it take as long as it takes to complete each one.

This is how this book will work best for you: Every morning (or most mornings, if that's possible), read the exercise you are working on and go through your day, taking that thought with you and applying it to everything you do, and continue to do that every day until you feel ready to move on to the next exercise.

One more thing; keep looking back on past exercises and refresh your mind with them in order to not forget them and make sure they are still being applied in your life. So, let's start now with our first exercise, and as I stated earlier, I also need to be constantly reminded of these things myself, so let us continue to work on them together:

Seek No-One's Approval

Jesus said we are to seek no man's approval. You may say 'yes, I understand that, but there surely must be times when we need to seek another's approval.' For example, if you were attending a job interview and you were one of a handful of applicants, surely then you would be looking for the approval of the interviewer.

OK. Let's now imagine that you weren't looking for the interviewer's approval. What would happen? You would give a very honest appraisal of yourself without trying to impress the interviewer and without letting your ego get in the way.

If the company you were considering joining had set expectations from their employees which you didn't match up to, then the job probably wouldn't be suitable for you anyway. However, if they were open-minded and listened to what you had to say from an unbiased and honest viewpoint, then you would probably prove to be an asset to them.

Without even realising it, we probably seek the approval of other people many times each day. So this exercise is to be aware whenever we do it and then think; the next time I'm in a similar situation, I will deal with it differently.

Just be honest and true to yourself. You may be amazed at how much more you will be respected. And if your new way of dealing with people meets up with opposition, don't be surprised, just realise that egos don't usually like being ignored.

Accept What You Cannot Change

This is about learning to accept every circumstance that comes your way, regardless of whether it is pleasant or not. In fact, let's take it a step further; not only accepting, but even seeing every circumstance as a form of blessing.

I believe that the reason we are here on this amazing planet and living this life is because we chose the experience. You might be thinking; 'I don't recall having made a choice in this matter,' but believe me, there is much more to you than meets the eye. Your personality and characteristics are just a small part of who you are. Your soul or higher self is the part of you which chose this ride, and it certainly does know what's best for you, even though you may not yet appreciate it.

On that subject, I am going to relate a short Zen story. It's about a man who owned a small piece of land where he lived with his family and they lived off the land. He owned two horses; in fact, his horses were his only possessions.

One day, someone left the gate to the field, where he kept his horses, open and the horses escaped. The man's neighbour, on hearing of the incident, said, "Oh what a tragedy, you've lost everything you owned, how sad." But the man said, "We'll see."

The very next day, the horses returned of their own accord, and lo and behold, they brought with them two more horses. The neighbour, on hearing the good news, said, "What a wonderful thing, you now have four horses."

Shortly after this, the man's son fell off one of the new horses and broke his leg while he was breaking it in. The neighbour immediately called and said, "What a tragedy that your poor son has broken his leg." And the man said, "We'll see."

Well a week or so later, the army were coming round all the farms in the area to conscript all the young men to take them to fight in a war, but they couldn't take the man's son because he had a broken leg, and it was later found out that all the young men that had been taken to fight in the war lost their lives.

Do you get the point? Every experience, be it pleasant, unpleasant, happy or sad, serves a purpose in your life. Every cloud has a silver lining. From every occurrence, be it favourable or unfavourable, there is a benefit. For every door that closes another one opens. Nothing is totally good or bad.

Let everyone we come into contact with see that we are satisfied with our lives, regardless of what we have to endure. We are satisfied simply to be experiencing all that this life offers us.

So this exercise is to try to accept everything which can't be changed. If it can't be changed, you are going to have to accept it anyway, so why resist?

Harm No-One

Of course, it's obvious that to cause deliberate harm to anyone is unacceptable in any society, but what about mental or psychological harm? It is so easy to hurt someone, often without even realising it. So it's very much worth our while to examine the way we treat others, and to think before we speak.

There are many people in this world who suffer with confidence problems and low self-esteem, just because, in the past, they've been put down or made to feel worthless.

When I had my clinics, I would often see a patient with a low self-esteem, and the first thing I said to them was, "Who in the past has told you that you are not good enough in one way or another?" And guess what: every time, without fail, they gave me a name. Putting someone down can be harmful to them and it is a very real form of abuse.

I've spoken about harm to people, but what about harm to animals? Once again, I'm sure you will say, "It's obvious that it is wrong to be cruel to animals."

So let's talk then about the meat trade: Animals are born and bred just for the purpose of feeding us with their meat. Well, that's not strictly true. Let me rephrase that statement; animals are born and bred for the purpose of making money for people in the meat trade.

I am not here saying it's wrong to eat meat, it is a personal choice, but it might be an enlightening thing for you to take a look at the meat trade, and then see how you feel about encouraging it to prosper.

In December 2011, I read a small book on the subject of advancing spiritually, and in this book, there were a couple of points made that I hadn't thought of before. Firstly, it mentioned the fact that animals (being far more sensitive than us) are aware that they are being led to their death, however humane the process may be. The book pointed out that the dense, low vibrational energy of the fear that the animals experience remains in the meat, and we eat that.

The points I just mentioned led me to make a decision to stop eating meat, which I did in January 2012. People ask me if I feel better since then and I think the answer to that question is obvious.

Of course, this development went right against the advice of my blood group teachings, because group 'O' (which I am) is considered to be the oldest blood group (the hunter/gatherer).

Maybe in early civilizations that was all they had to eat, but as I said earlier (in the chapter *A Word About Evolution*), we adapt very well to our circumstances and our environment, so with plenty of protein from other sources and the right mental attitude, I've found it to be rather easy, especially as my conscience is now clear on that subject. Although I must point out that, if you have decided to become vegetarian or especially vegan, make sure you get plenty of vitamin B12; there is the possibility of many unpleasant side effects resulting from a B12 deficiency.

Having said all of the above, I do not judge anyone for doing what they believe to be right, but perhaps your conscience has now been pricked. Always remember though; you are free to make your own choices in life.

Judge No-One

This is a big one. You may be thinking, 'I'm not judgemental', but is this really true? I believe it could take most of us the rest of our lives to become totally non-judgemental, and we would still need more time.

Judgementalism is really a form of Dualism. So what is Dualism? It is the 'them and us' syndrome; Conservative and Labour, Republican and Democrat, Catholic and Protestant, Arab and Jew, Good and Bad, Right and Wrong.

Politicians and religious leaders just don't get it! To believe that God is on your side is pure arrogance, and it means that neither side is right. Jesus pointed this out on so many occasions, yet so-called Christian religions are among the most dualistic organisations in society today.

You would do well to take into consideration the words of Jesus in Mathew 5:44; 'Love your enemies and bless those who curse you, do good to those who hate you and pray for those who despitefully use and persecute you.'

We live in a totally dualistic society and we will never even begin to understand the true meaning of peace until that all changes.

One person's right is another person's wrong, one person's belief is another person's disbelief, one person's pleasure is another person's displeasure. Who is right and who is wrong? Zen teachings tell us that there is no right or wrong, there just is. Or to put it another way; it is what it is.

Taking sides is nothing but Dualism, which leads to Judgementalism, and none of that will lead you down the path of true contentment. Jesus said; 'Judge not that you not be judged, for with what judgement you judge, you will be judged, and with the measure you use, it will be measured back to you.' (Matthew 7:1, 2)

This could easily be interpreted as a warning of punishment from above, but what Jesus was saying here is that the universe is a mirror; what you give out bounces right back to you because you created it in the first place.

Separation, competitiveness and divisiveness are all signs of dualism, so let's go through some typical examples of dualism in our everyday lives.

Beware of Duality

The following chapter looks at some everyday ways in which duality rears its ugly head in today's society, especially in the western world.

Avoid Competitiveness

There's nothing wrong with a good challenge, but when does it become dualistic? When we feel the need to be better than our opponent. When we fight to win. When we find it difficult to accept that someone is better than us. When we gloat in pride after being triumphant.

This is when the ego has become involved. So, if you can enjoy a competition without the need to win, if you can just simply enjoy the taking part, then it can truly be called healthy competition.

Uniforms

Wearing a uniform may be a simple form of being identified, but it can also be a form of duality which in this modern world can be impossible to avoid. Probably our first uniform is our school one. It has obvious advantages, for example, it's very helpful to be able to identify children when they're out of school.

But it is also used as a form of duality. Sports day is a typical example of this, and it is probably one of the first experiences in our young lives when our egos are encouraged to flourish.

In our adult life, uniforms are often part of our everyday experience. If we go to a dinner party or function, we are expected to wear the customary black tie attire; have you ever noticed how people look distastefully at the odd one or two people who choose not to conform?

There is also the issue of morals; if a female decides to wear a short skirt or dress, notice how much she is often stared at in a judgemental way by other females who consider it to be immoral, those who are very often having an affair with someone else's husband.

Then, of course, there is the uniform which goes with the job; policeman, fireman, ambulance worker, sports person, or a member of the armed forces. The point is that there is nothing wrong with wearing a uniform for the purpose of being identified, even though that still sets us apart and is dualistic by nature, but we should remember that we live in a dualistic world where it is impossible to practise total oneness.

The problem arises when the use of the uniform goes further and becomes an expression of the ego; the word proudness comes to mind here.

Politics

How many times have you heard a politician argue the case for his party, regardless of the point being made? When did you last hear a politician admit that his party is going about things the wrong way? We only seem to experience this when a politician deflects and joins an opposing party after too many issues have arisen that he or she just can't live with any longer. But up until that point in time, he or she has continued to be loyal to their party, regardless of whether or not they agree with every policy.

The mere fact that both sides always have an argument to put forward surely suggests that they are both right in different ways. Of course, the problem with that argument is that they are also both wrong in different ways, because there is right and wrong in every argument.

The fact of the matter though is that because they both refuse to listen to the other sides' point of view, it makes them dualistic in nature, because paradoxically, there is no complete right or wrong.

Religion

This is a subject which could, if allowed, take up a whole book. How can different religions be at loggerheads when there truly is only one religion? "What religion is that?" You may well ask; is my religion the right one?

Well if it's doesn't have a label and it involves living in love and peace, then perhaps you are on the right track. Any organisation, be it political, business or religious, is taking you in completely the wrong direction if it encourages or endorses war or violence. How much plainer could it be?

Jesus said; 'All who take the sword will perish by the sword.' (Matthew 26:52)

The words of Jesus don't seem to be followed in this regard, despite the fact that so-called Christian religions profess to be guided by him. This is sheer hypocrisy.

Of course, the following argument always raises its head in this regard: If everyone thought like us and refused to fight, we would be in a very serious state of bondage. No, if everyone thought like us, there would be no war.

Did Jesus fight to save his life when he was being put to death? No, instead he forgave his perpetrators. He was showing us that love is more important than taking up arms against our fellow humans, even if they take up arms against us. He showed us that this life is not all there is and that if we lived a peaceful and non-violent life, our reward would be great.

It would be very beneficial for individual members of the church, clergy and lay people to re-think the principles of Jesus (repeated many times in many different ways in the scriptures). Read his words again, with regard to taking up arms, and then ask yourself; does my church follow Jesus' example?

Is it possible that they are the very organisations that Jesus was talking about when he said in Matthew 15:8-9: 'These people draw near to me with their mouth and honour me with their lips, but their heart is far from me. In vain they worship me, teaching as doctrines the commandments of men.'

Then in Matthew 15:14, he said, 'Let them alone, they are blind leaders of the blind, and if the blind leads the blind, both will fall into a ditch.' I wonder if that ditch could possibly be interpreted as the crumbling of church attendances and the selling off of church buildings in modern times.

On that subject, it is worth asking yourself; does my church follow the example of Jesus, or does it teach the commands of mere men in high places?

It may be beneficial to re-think your whole standpoint and consider making some serious changes in your life.

Materialism

Spending your life thinking about what you can gain in a material sense is futile. You came into the world with nothing, and you leave it with nothing. So what have you gained? Nothing (nothing material or worthwhile anyway). But hopefully you will have gained much in the way of wisdom and spirituality; those are the things that really matter.

Jesus made this clear in Matthew 6:19-21, when he said, 'Do not lay up for yourselves treasures on earth where moth and rust destroy and where thieves break in and steal, for where your treasure is, your heart will be also.'

And that leads me to talk about a form of materialism which needs our serious consideration:

Attachment

I'm going to start this section by telling you a short Zen story: There was a man who was walking along a riverbank, and the terrain was rough, making it very difficult for him to walk. When he looked over to the other side of the river, he saw the ground was very smooth, which would make his journey so much easier. So he thought, 'I must find a way to cross this deep river.'

After some thought, he decided to bind together with reeds some logs and fallen tree branches, and he made himself a raft. Then using an old branch as a punt, he made his way safely over to the other side.

He was very pleased with the raft he had made, so pleased in fact that he thought it might come in handy in the future, so he carried it on his back for the rest of his journey.

Do you get it? He became so attached to his raft that he actually allowed it to weigh him down, resulting in his journey becoming even more difficult than it was at the start.

Do you do that? Do you carry baggage that's slowing down your progress on your spiritual journey? Do you find it difficult to let go of objects, ideas, or even people that hinder you on your spiritual journey? Any form of un-needed clutter will block your energy and slow down your progress.

The less we attach ourselves to possessions, ideas, outcomes and people, the easier our lives will be.

Practises We Would All Do Well to Develop

Show Kindness

We all love it when someone shows kindness to us; it brightens up our day and makes us feel that we would like to do the same for someone else. But the trouble is that we are often too selective with our giving of kindness. We show kindness only to people we know and like. But don't we feel good after we've helped someone who needed assistance;

the typical good deed for the day syndrome? What ever happened to that?

So this exercise is to show kindness, not only to a selected few, but to everyone we come into contact with in our daily lives; a smile costs nothing, and you may be pleasantly surprised by the response you get.

However, if you meet with hostility it just means that the person you are trying to show kindness to isn't, for one reason or another, in a receptive mood at that time. That's OK, just smile and move on.

Stop Worrying

Let's start here with the wise words of Jesus when he said; 'Do not worry about your life, what you will eat or what you will drink; nor about your body, what you will put on. Is not life more than food and the body more than clothing? Which of you by worrying can add one cubit to his stature? Do not worry about tomorrow, for tomorrow will have enough troubles of its own.' (Matthew 6:25, 27, 34)

Spending your time worrying about what might happen in your life is futile. Living in the moment is the only way to gain contentment. The past is history, and the only benefits you can gain by thinking about it is to learn lessons from your mistakes, not to punish yourself for those mistakes.

Fear is a more intense form of worry; so it would be a wise thing to take heed of a Zen teaching which says; 'What you fear you bring to you.' In other words, thinking is an energetic projection, and we are all creators of our own destiny, so if we spend time thinking about a fearful situation, we are actually creating that situation in our lives.

As I'm sure you are aware; worrying about a problem will do absolutely nothing towards resolving it, but calmly considering a way to deal with it will. So this exercise is to stop worrying, and if you have a problem which you can do nothing to resolve, go back to the exercise; *Go with The Flow* and just accept it.

Don't Make Promises You Can't Keep

This section could probably be more accurate if it was just simply titled *Don't Make Promises*. No one knows for sure how they are going to feel about something in the future. No one knows how much their circumstances are going to change. What if you make a promise to someone, and then wish you'd never made it? What will you do? Will you keep your promise and feel constant regret and wish you'd never made it in the first place, or will you break your promise and say, "I'm very sorry but things have changed since I made my promise?"

Personally, I don't feel comfortable making promises to anyone unless I am absolutely sure, because I don't know if circumstances are going to always remain the same. Of course, that now puts me on dodgy ground, because of one of the most important promises that people make in their lives are the wedding vows, the promises that are made in the marriage ceremony.

So, am I saying that it is wrong to marry? Certainly not, I am no judge of right and wrong. I just think that it is not something that should be taken lightly.

With over 50% of marriages in the western world ending in divorce, my point is made. People change, circumstances change, so it's only to be expected. If those people hadn't made those promises in the first place, they wouldn't be breaking them if, after a period of time, they went their own ways for whatever reason.

This now brings us to a moral issue; is it not immoral for a couple to live together and possibly procreate if they are not married? Are they as the cliché says, 'living in sin'? Who said so?

Let us now look at marriage for what it actually is: history tells us that a marriage's primary purpose was to bind women to men, and thus guarantee that a man's children were truly his biological heirs.

In times past, through marriage, a woman became a man's property. This process was then adopted by the church, which, along with the government at the time decided to make it a legal requirement. So from that time on, it was considered to be a sin to cohabit with someone you weren't married to.

Before you condemn someone who just wants to live their lives without a legally binding contract, please ask yourself one question; do you believe in your heart that it is truly immoral to live this way, or have you been programmed or conditioned by judgemental religious organisations to believe it?

To me, marriage is a joining together of two people who wish to live their lives together and I don't believe you have to sign contracts or make lifetime promises to prove your devotion to someone. However, if you are absolutely sure that this person is the right one and you want to show it, then getting married can be a wonderful thing. It's not a moral issue; it is purely a matter of preference.

One other thing which may be worth considering is the female's feelings; women often feel the need to be protected (before you pull the equal rights card, I'm not talking about all women, just the majority as I have experienced them. You have to be so careful not to offend these days).

One of the main reasons for people not getting on together is because of expectations. You know the kind of thing; 'I don't understand why she did that', 'I think he owes me an apology', 'Why is she always late?', 'He totally blanked me when I saw him in the town today', 'I expect better treatment than this.' I think a whole book could be written on the subject of expectations alone.

Please keep in mind that you are a person who is in touch with your sixth sense (your spiritual side). Most people you come across in everyday life are only aware that they have five senses. Of course, everyone has a sixth sense which could guide them through this life so much more easily, but sadly, they don't often experience it because it has been pushed deep within by their ego, so we need to have patience with them.

With no expectations, there are no disappointments, and with no disappointments, there is contentment. The secret is to be as kind and generous as you can, and to expect nothing back in return. If you don't have expectations, you are showing them a perfect example of sixth sensory practise.

However, if people haven't reached your level of understanding it's a waste of time trying to help them to understand. Accept the fact that they are not at this moment in time ready to hear what you have to say; it's a bit like trying to feed a baby with a hearty meal, or as Jesus so appropriately put it: 'it's like throwing pearls before swine.' (Matthew 7:6)

So for that reason, please keep in mind one of my favourite sayings: 'To a believer no evidence is required, but to a non-believer no evidence will suffice.'

With that in mind then; *Don't Expect Anything from Anyone.*

Avoid Complaining

I am not here trying to say that you should not send back a meal if it isn't what you ordered or take back an item that is faulty. What I am saying though is that many people today seem to make a point of complaining about almost everything. That leads to a rather miserable existence which lacks any sort of happiness or contentment.

Another thing which is regularly complained about is BOREDOM. I'm sure you've heard it many times; 'I'm bored', 'there's nothing to do'. Well I'm sure that we, on this spiritual journey never need to get bored. There is always something to learn or do, so let's set an example to those who complain of being bored. Let them see that our lives are full, full of contentment.

Avoid Gossip

Before we talk about someone's weak points, we should ask ourselves; would I still be saying this if the person I am talking about was present? If the answer to that question is no, (apart from when you are trying to genuinely help them), then you are gossiping.

In today's society, it seems that almost everybody spends time talking about other people, often people they are close to. Gossip is like a cancerous disease and we would do well to constantly keep ourselves in check in this regard. Imagine how bad you would feel if that person overheard what you were saying.

So, if we refuse to get involved in unkind small talk, we will certainly feel good about it. It takes a brave action to say to someone who wants to gossip, 'I'm sorry but I tend to avoid talking about people unless something good is being said', you will probably only have to say that once, they will definitely get the message.

You will either set a good example and have made a stand for the future and be respected more, or you will receive a hostile response which will mean those people will keep away from you, but that's fine as well; it will solve your problem anyway because you won't be exposed to their future gossip.

Avoid Mental Criticism

There is nothing wrong with healthy criticism. So what then is unhealthy criticism? It is criticism which hasn't been invited, hasn't been called for. You may think being critical of someone is just another form of gossiping. Well actually it is, but the kind of criticism I'm here referring to is the kind which you don't speak, but the kind that you think.

I added in this section because I recently became aware of my own weaknesses in this regard. We show kindness and compassion as part of who we are, but what about what we think? I found myself being overly, mentally critical of people's words and actions. It's so easy to think negative thoughts about people, but in reality, it is nothing more than judgementalism, which is, as I've stated earlier, just another form of dualism.

Thank goodness I realised and am now working on this. I find the best way to deal with mental criticism is to immediately correct yourself every time you find yourself doing it. My way of dealing with it is to say in my mind: 'stop criticising', and for me that does the trick.

Whenever your mind seems to be taking over, take it out of the driver's seat and put it in the back. Another way to silence your mind is to say, "I wonder what my next thought is going to be." It works every time for me, because the mind hates to be observed, it prefers to stay in the shadows.

Walk Tall

As the song says, 'Walk tall, walk straight and look the world right in the eye.' But walking straight and tall does not mean being proud. Pride is of the ego. You walk straight and tall because you are confident, not ashamed about what you believe. You walk straight and tall because you have nothing to hide and you feel good because of this. Your head is upright, your shoulders are back, your chest is out and your back is straight.

Why is this so? It is because you are privileged to understand what this life is about and what your purpose in it is, and you want others to see how contented you are, in fact that's all you need to do; there is no need for preaching, just being who you are.

When other people see this contentment, and only if they are ready for change, they will want to know your secret, they will want some of what you have. But be warned, if they are driven only by their ego they will not be impressed by your confidence.

So this exercise is 'Walk tall, walk straight and look the world right in the eye.'

Turn Your Eyes Inward

Yes, this exercise is to examine ourselves, examine our thoughts, desires, actions and more importantly our motives, and to see just how much our ego is playing a part in our daily lives.

The only way we'll help to make a difference in this world is to stop looking at the faults of everyone else and start looking at our own misgivings.

Jesus said in Matthew 7:3-5; 'Why do you look at the speck in your brother's eye, but do not consider the plank in your own eye? Or how can you say to your brother, "Let me remove the speck from your eye", when there is a plank in your own eye. Hypocrite! First remove the plank from your own eye, and then you will see clearly to remove the speck from your brother's eye.'

Whenever an act of terrorism takes place, the country or group that has been attacked looks for someone to blame, whereas the first thing that would help to avoid further action like this would be for them to look for the flaws in their own society.

Instead of digging our heels in and assuming that we are right and they are wrong, it would be far more beneficial to look firstly at *why* the attack took place or what grievances those people have against you and why. Then honest and truthful dialogue is the only successful way to deal with the problem. You cannot and will never be able to make peace with war. Buddhist teachings say: 'blood stains cannot be removed with more blood and resentment cannot be removed with more resentment, it can only be removed by forgetting it.'

Peace is not something you can work for or strive to attain, you cannot force peace into being, it (just like sleep) is a passive state and it is the result of non-action. You don't work for peace; you just live a passive life and then allow it to happen. You cannot make peace with war.

If only the politicians, governments and religious leaders turned their eyes inwards and looked at their own faults, this world would be a far more peaceful place.

But as you examine yourself and your motives, keep one thing in mind: it is not beneficial to judge yourself in a harsh or overly critical way, or to punish yourself for your past mistakes. This would be destructive and lead to feelings of inferiority or guilt.

The whole purpose of turning our eyes inward and examining ourselves is to learn from our mistakes and to see how we can improve and beneficially affect the future. This exercise is an observation, not a moral judgement of ourselves (there's already too much moral judging going on in the world as it is).

Be It

It is not necessary or even beneficial to spread the word of your new understanding, in fact it will probably be met with ridicule from those who are on a different level of understanding. So how can you help others to see the amazing new truth that you have found? The answer is simple; don't talk about it or preach it, just *be it*.

The very best way to teach is by example, so by just doing your best to live your life as you believe it should be lived is by far the best way to teach. All you need to do is live a peaceful life and let your contentment be your witness. Jesus said, 'Blessed are the peacemakers, for they shall be called the children of God.' (Matthew 5:9)

And when you find it becomes difficult in a world full of hostility, find a like-minded person and spend some time with them. It will give you a boost and help keep you encouraged. If you don't have anyone who sees life as you do, then read a book or go on the internet and find a way to keep close to someone who sees life as you do. There's always a way to keep close to like-minded people.

Pray or Meditate Regularly

This is a really interesting one. What does it mean to pray? If you listen to the world's religions, you would think you need to pray to God for forgiveness and to ask Him to protect you and your loved ones, but as I mentioned back in the earlier pages of this book; God is not a person, but love. How can you pray to love?

God is in everything loving and kind, so when we show love and kindness, we are actually part of God, and there is certainly no need to pray to ourselves.

And why do we need to be forgiven for our so-called sins, when we came here partly for the purpose of making those mistakes and experiencing human life, positives and negatives? And why should we and our loved ones be protected with the exclusion of everyone else in the world?

Prayer is not a one-way transmission, asking for something, then waiting to see if we get a favourable answer, or in the worst-case scenario, never getting an answer. So let's get one thing straight; prayer is not begging for forgiveness from a higher entity, any more than it is an asking for our lives to improve. It is a way of opening our mind and accepting wisdom and guidance from the universe, the all-loving universe of which we are all a part. It is more of a two-way street than a one-way one.

So is it wrong to ask anything of the universe? Not at all, but it does depend on what you ask for. Nothing you ask for should be out of selfishness or for personal gain.

It is a good thing for us to show our gratitude, and ask for guidance as to how we can be of more assistance in helping others to see the light, then accepting whatever comes our way in this life.

Meditation is possibly the new label for prayer, because in this doubting world it seems to be more accepted. But *what is* prayer or meditation? It is communication; your way of connecting to the love of the universe. The universe is a mirror, so what you give out is what you receive (what you yourself created).

These days meditation is recommended in most spiritual books, but how to do it can be a very difficult thing; we are told to relax and open our mind, but in all honesty I always found this to be very difficult, especially as I have a busy mind, like many people these days.

So something worth trying is recommended in Richard Rohr's book *The Naked Now*. It suggests that we try a walking meditation; taking a walk (preferably down a hill), then trying to time our breathing with our steps (probably between six and ten steps as we breathe in, then the same amount of steps as we breathe out). It's worth practising that before you move on to the next stage.

When you have a comfortable rhythm going, say a chosen word as you inhale, then another chosen word on the out breath (the choice of words is up to you). Richard uses the words beauty and back.

Then on the return journey (up the hill), the breathing becomes more challenged, but after a while it can become an easy routine. As you do it, try to keep the rhythm going; walking, breathing, and saying your chosen words at the beginning of each in and out breath.

I personally found that the word love on the in *and* out breath works best for me. You don't have to speak out loud, just think your words. As you breathe in and say the word love, look to the sky, or mountains, or a forest (or in fact anything natural) and imagine breathing in the love of the universe. Then as you breathe out, either look again at that natural scene and imagine sending that love right back to the universe, or perhaps send your love to other humans (you don't have to know them, anyone will do), they are probably in need of love far more right now than the plants and trees are.

After a while of practising the walking meditation, you probably won't even need to say the words anymore; it's your intention that counts. You can take in and give out love just as easily without having to speak or even think words.

Hopefully this technique will open our mind and prevent us being troubled by mundane, everyday thoughts which our ego would love to fill our minds with. Also we will hopefully gain inspiration whilst walking, and it's a great way to connect with the love of the universe.

Another form of meditation which can be beneficial is to do daily Qi Gong exercises (already mentioned earlier in this book). After regular practise, you could connect with the power of the universe and do your physical exercise at the same time.

So, this exercise is to connect with the love of the universe at least once every day (by whatever means suits you), and to open your mind in a loving way. Believe me you will be given everything you need, and all your questions will be answered in one way or another.

Read Other Books

Please do this as well as reading this book. There is a massive amount of knowledge and wisdom to be gained by doing this; in fact, much of my inspiration is triggered by reading books which get me wondering about the important things in life.

Then when I have questions I need answered, I simply open my mind for the answers, and so far I have been blessed with answers galore, enough in fact to write this very book.

Slow Down

In this modern world, everything seems to be geared to speed; faster transport, more motorways, faster cars, faster internet connection, timesaving devices home and self-service checkouts at the supermarket. The irony though, is that the faster our world becomes, the longer everything seems to take to get done. We seem to be running around like headless chickens, but what is at the end of it all? Death. Yes, that's right; we are all doing nothing more than hurrying to our death.

So this exercise is to make a special effort to slow down. Some excellent advice is given by John Ortberg in his book *The Life You've Always Wanted*. He suggests that, for a period of time we train ourselves to slow down by purposely choosing the longest queue in the supermarket, by driving in the slowest lane on the motorway, and by eating our meals slowly and properly chewing every mouthful.

You may well be thinking; "I don't have the time to take things more slowly, my life is busy and hectic." Well it might then be worthwhile to take stock of what it is that we fill our lives with; perhaps less time wasted on unnecessary pursuits could free up some quality time to spend on the things that really matter. Perhaps then we could leave home a little earlier and allow more time to get to our destination or spend some more time on quality pursuits.

Let's not forget that, years ago when we didn't have the time-saving devices such as washing machines, dishwashers and cars, everything important still got done and people often seemed to enjoy social gatherings as well.

The hurrying in our everyday lives is a disease of modern society and it would be of great benefit for us to avoid it as much as possible and save the rushing for real emergencies.

Declutter

According to Feng Shui, we will never experience contentment if we have clutter in our lives. But exactly what am I referring to when I speak of clutter? I am referring to clutter of the mind, body and the environment in which we live.

Energy needs to flow freely if it is to lead to a peaceful life. It can't flow freely if our mind is full of mental rubbish, it can't flow freely if our body is full of pollutants, and neither can it flow freely if our environment is full of clutter.

It would serve us very well to examine the energy blockages we cause in our mind, such as negative thoughts and things that do not serve us for the good. It would serve us very well to examine the junk we put into our body, and it would also serve us very well to examine the clutter in our home or work environment.

A good question to ask ourselves on all these counts is: 'What can I clean out of my mind, body and environment that will help the energy to flow more freely?' It really works; in Japan, companies call in Feng Shui experts to advise them on de-cluttering the work environment, and they swear by the results.

Go with the Flow

A common saying, but how powerful this is. If you learn to go with the flow, your life will change for the better, drastically. Going with the flow means avoiding resistance. That may sound simple, but let's consider just how much we resist things in our everyday lives.

Every time you are involved in an argument which gets heated, you are resisting. Every time you refuse to accept something you cannot change, you are resisting. Every time you fight an illness, you are resisting. Am I saying that it is not good to resist? Yes, surrender is sweet.

Resistance doesn't cure illness, it causes it. The Oriental way of looking after your health is to help the body's bioenergy to flow more smoothly, not to resist or fight it. Feng Shui teaches us to organise our lives to avoid energy blockages (resistance) in our lives.

The more we resist going with the flow, the more our lives will be unhealthy, in mind and body. So this exercise is to avoid resistance as much as possible, but don't try too hard because that in itself is a form of resistance.

Am I saying that we should agree with everything everyone says and allow ourselves to be manipulated? Not at all; just because you are determined to go with the flow and avoid resistance, that doesn't mean you are putty in everyone's hands. You have a mind of your own and certain principles which guide you in life, and that is commendable.

There is a big difference between making your beliefs known and having a heated argument with someone. Remember; it is not necessary to make people aware that you are right, even if you know you are. If they don't want to listen, don't waste your energy trying to reason with them.

And keep in mind that if the majority were always right, the world would be a far better place. On the contrary, it's more often than not the wisest course to do the opposite of what the majority do. This was born out by Jesus when he said in Matthew 7:13-14; 'Enter by the narrow gate, for wide is the gate and broad is the way that leads to destruction, and there are many who go in by it. And narrow is the gate and difficult is the way that leads to life, and there are few who find it.'

So this exercise is to follow the Oriental practice of Wu Wei; remain as calm as possible and avoid resistance. For each set of circumstances you face, ask yourself; "Am I going with the flow, or am I resisting?" You may be very surprised at how much resistance you have been creating in your life in the past.

Open Your Mind

Don't be afraid to change your mind about what you believe, even if you've believed it the whole of your life. In fact, if you still have the same values and beliefs now that you have always had, it means that your mind is closed and you haven't matured spiritually.

If we listen to everything everyone tells us and then chew it over, not with our mind (ego) but with our heart (conscience), we will often change the way we feel about things for the better.

Are you too proud to admit that you were wrong? Does your ego prevent you from saying to someone, "I thought about what you said and it has helped me to see things differently now."

Constantly defending ourselves when we are challenged is never going to help us to become wise. We only have to watch a political debate to see each side just trying to give a good answer to the challenge and never seeing the point of view of the other person. In other words, each side doing their utmost to protect their ego. The world has more than enough intelligent fools, let's not join them.

So this exercise is to listen to what people say before making judgements, and then change your mind and your beliefs when a better way is shown to you. And by the way, if you get accused of always changing your mind, take that as a compliment, it means you are learning and moving on, it's far better than being stuck in your ways.

Listen and Learn

If we refuse to listen, we refuse to learn, and our lives will go nowhere. Should we listen to everything that people try to tell us? Yes. If we disagree with the principles of others, there will always be something we can take away with us, even if that something is only confirmation of why we didn't agree in the first place.

Nothing in this world is completely right or completely wrong, so why not listen carefully to what others say, then see if there's anything of value that we can take with us.

Live for Today

As I said at the beginning of this book; the past is nothing more than a memory and the future is nothing more than supposition. So what are we left with? That's right, the present moment is all there actually is, the only real thing in this life.

If the average person added up all the time they were thinking about the past and the future, there would be very little time left to think about the present moment, so let's now make a point of living for today. Start putting in place the beginnings of the things you've been putting off, the things you've talked about doing, but never actually started. Remember the saying 'Tomorrow never comes.'

Of course, we have to plan for the future to some extent; if we don't book that holiday in advance, or book our seats in the theatre, we won't be able to go. The secret is to not be anxious about future events, but to make the best of today.

Also, thinking about the past can be beneficial. All the mistakes we made are a wonderful learning opportunity for us to avoid making those mistakes again, and all the good times are worth remembering so we can repeat them often. It only becomes a problem when we either dread the future or allow the effects of past events to take away our contentment in the present.

So let's make a point of reducing dramatically our thoughts of past and future, by only focussing on the positive ones. That way we'll free up a lot more time for thinking about today. Why not do something today which is the beginning of something you've been putting off? Trust me, you'll feel very good about it.

Set an Example

We are all human, all made of the same stuff and all have the same rights. Just because a person or group of

people act in a different way, that doesn't make them sub-
standard or of lesser value than us. It doesn't even mean they
are wrong, it just means that they think differently, and that
may be because of the way they've been programmed and
conditioned.

Again you might say, "I'm not programmed or
conditioned by anyone, I make my own decisions and
judgements in this life." But how true is that? Think about
what you wear, how you speak, where you shop, and even
how you hold your knife and fork. Yes, we have all been
influenced by the environment we grew up in, and it's all
based on what we've been told is right or wrong, but how
much of that is actually true?

The person we become is made up of many differing
influences; the way our parents taught us, the friends we
associate with, the influences from our siblings or the people
we work or socialise with, the political party we belong to
and the religion or indoctrination we are exposed to. All
these things and many more go to making up the person we
become.

If we live a life of terrorism and kill people because of
our religious beliefs, that doesn't make us wicked, it just
means that we carry out wicked acts, in fact many people
that carry out these acts of violence do it because they
sincerely believe it is with the approval of their God, and out
of those who judge them to be wicked, how many of *those*
would be prepared to lay down their life for the sake of their
beliefs?. So who are the more sincere ones here?

If we are a paedophile or rapist, it's because we have
such strong sexual feelings, and we are too weak to control
them. The paedophile or rapist knows fully well that it is

wrong to exercise such vile control over another person (especially one who is unable to protect themselves), but they simply ignore their conscience.

I heard a convicted paedophile being interviewed on the radio recently, and he said he was glad he was in prison because he wouldn't trust himself on the outside. Is that not the words of a sincere person? Would those who want to beat him up, or even put him to death be so honest? I wonder.

Of one thing I'm certain; these people didn't choose to have those feelings. Don't you think they would give anything in order to be free of those feelings and live a normal life? Aren't we lucky then that we don't have those degraded feelings?

Please don't think I'm saying it's OK to be a person who does such vile things, I am not. But it would be far better to help a weak person to see things in a different light than it would to judge them as being inferior to us. As I mentioned earlier in this book, Jesus once said, 'Let the one without sin cast the first stone.' We all have the ability to forgive; in fact, we will *have* to forgive if we want to experience true contentment.

So this exercise is: show kindness and equality to everyone you meet, regardless of whom they are or what they do. That doesn't mean we should condone or encourage bad behaviour, it simply means (in the words of Jesus to those who put him to death): 'Forgive them for they no not what they do' (Luke 23:34). And the best way to teach them is to be a shining light in their presence.

Of course, being a shining light will also attract attention, which in turn could easily attract hostility from threatened egos, but be encouraged by the words of Jesus when he said. "Blessed are they which are persecuted for righteousness sake, for they will inherit the kingdom of heaven" (Matthew 5:10-12).

And; 'Whoever hears these sayings of mine and does them, I will liken him to a wise man who built his house on the rock. And the rain descended, the floods came and the winds blew and beat on that house, and it did not fall for it was founded on the rock. But everyone who hears these sayings of mine and does not do them will be like a foolish man who built his house on the sand. And the rain descended, the floods came and the winds blew and beat on that house, and it fell, and great was its fall.' (Matthew 7:24-27)

The biggest problem in this world is ignorance, and that's not a crime; it is a lack of understanding. So let's make it our job to help those who are ignorant to the truth, to understand, not by judging them to be inferior, but by setting them an example of how to find true contentment.

Conclusion

I hope through the pages of this book, I have touched on a few meaningful points which will help you to see things in a different way and encourage you to accept change, however small.

Also, I hope you will be helped to change circumstances in your life which will be of benefit, not only to yourself, but also the people you share your life with.